I0512420

FERRET COLORING BOOK

CRYSTAL
COLORING BOOKS

ISBN-13: 978-1987647181
ISBN-10: 1987647181

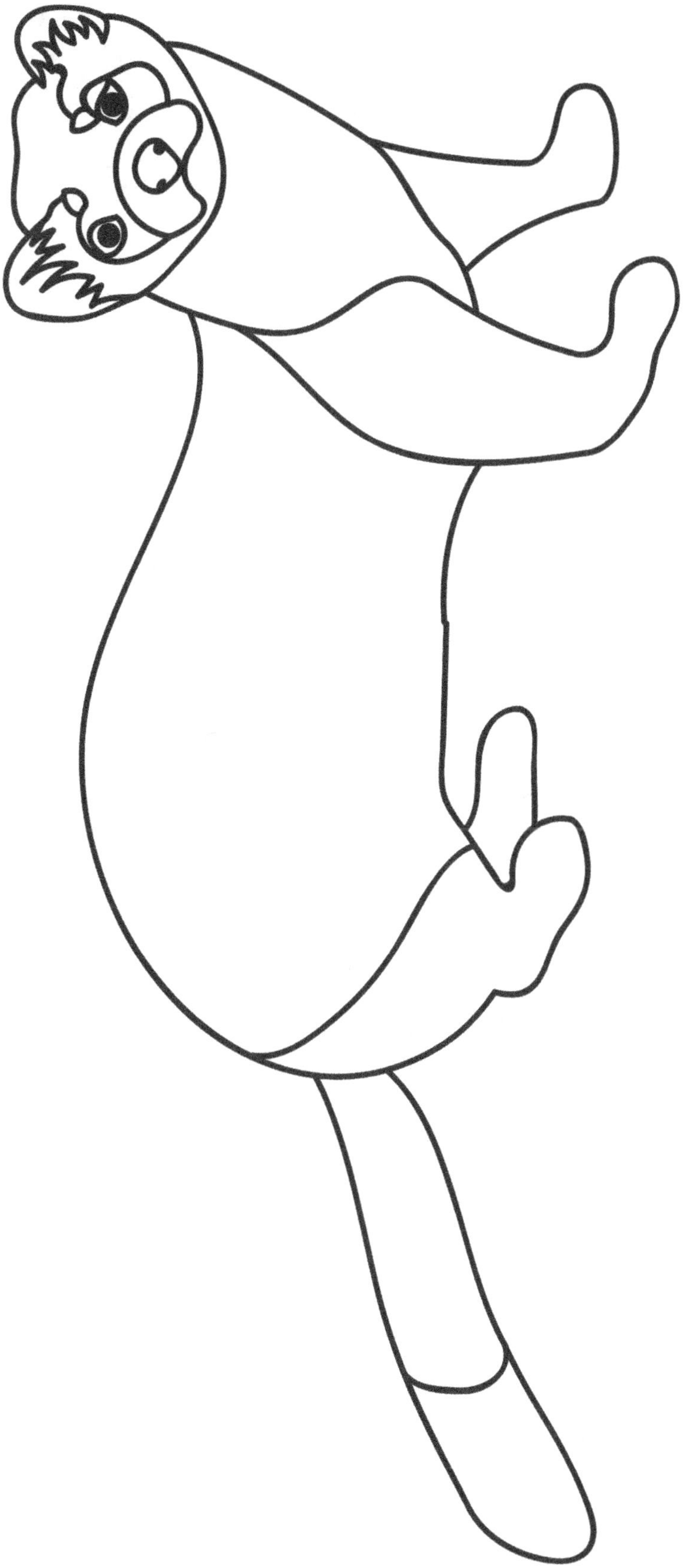

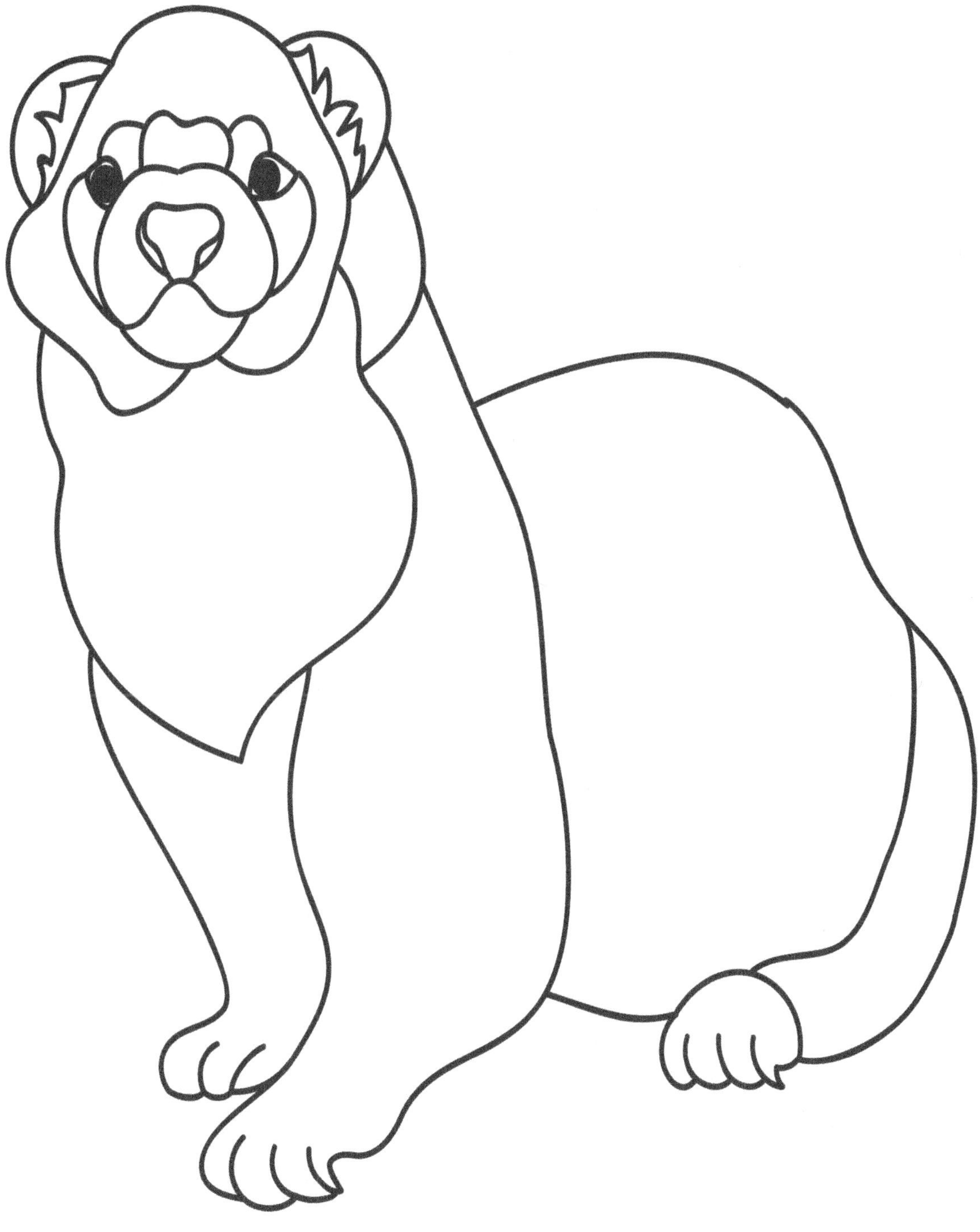

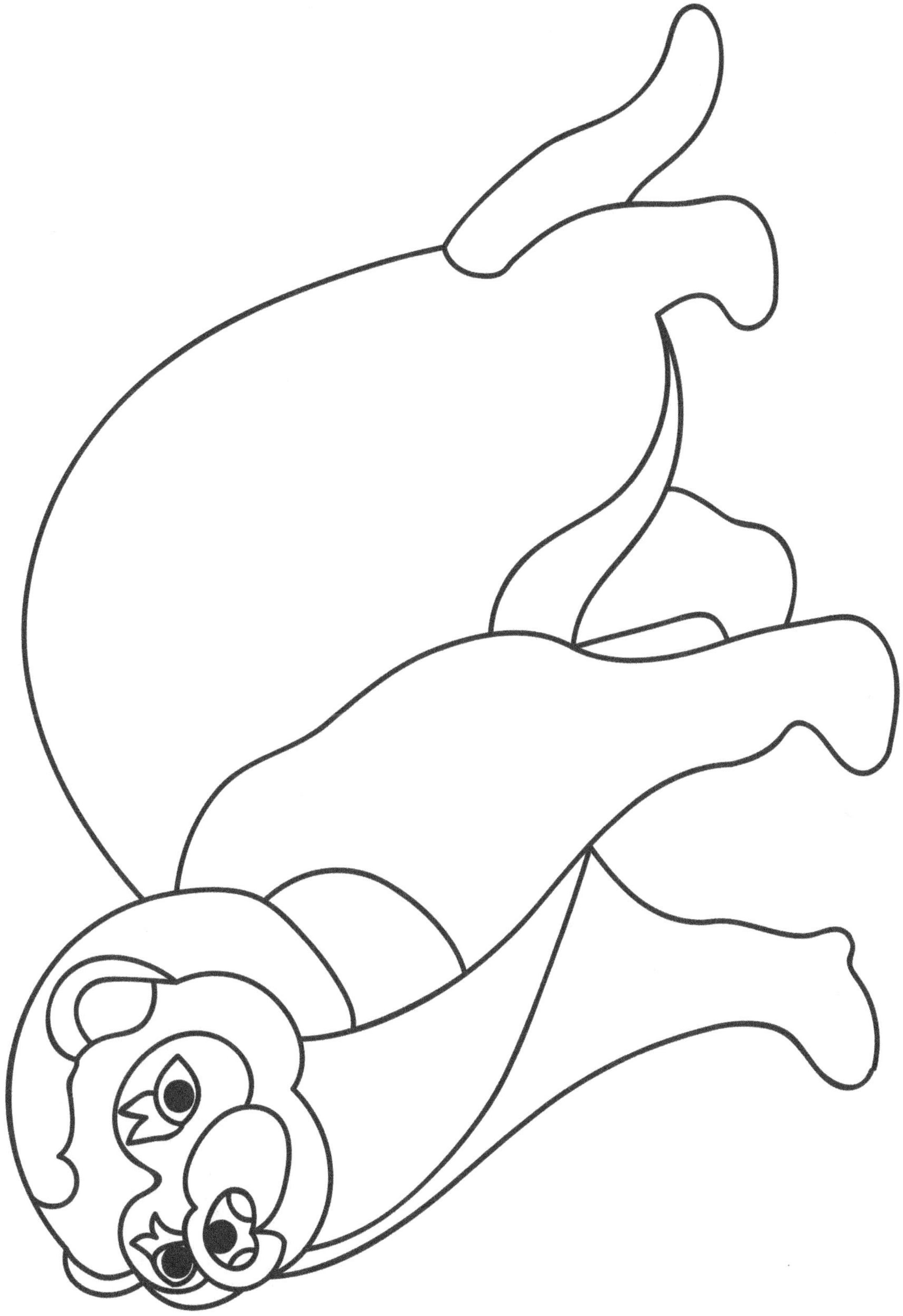

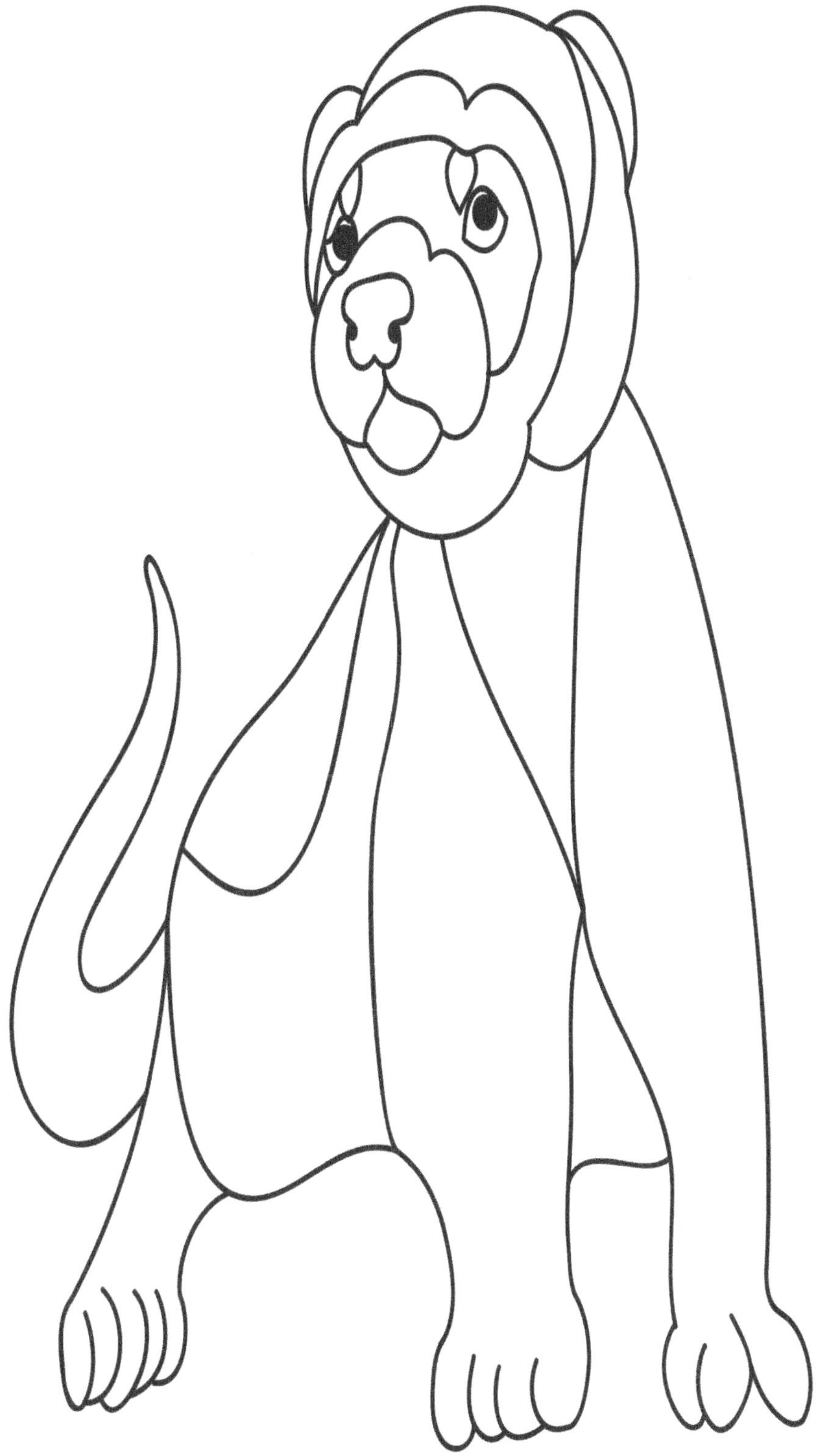

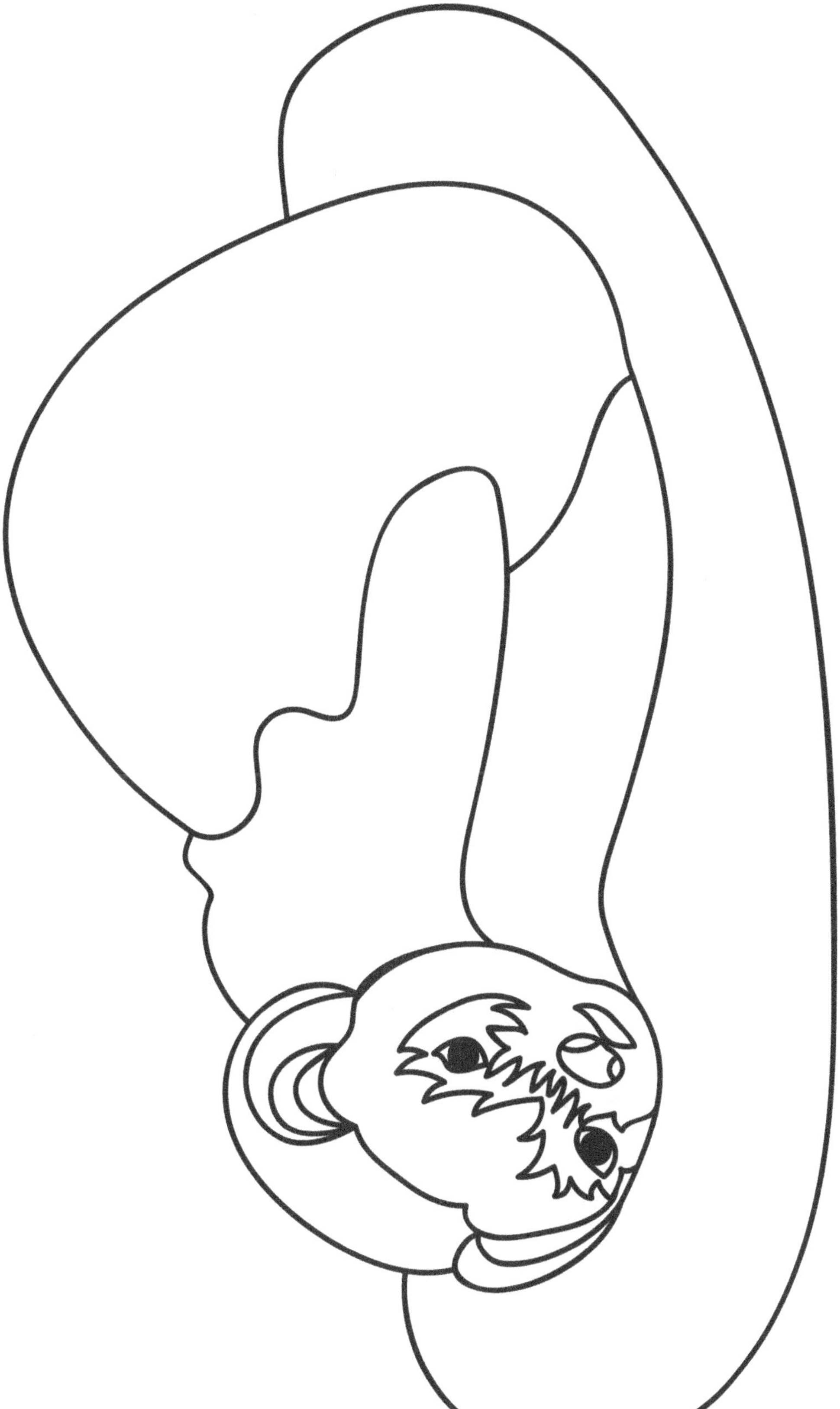

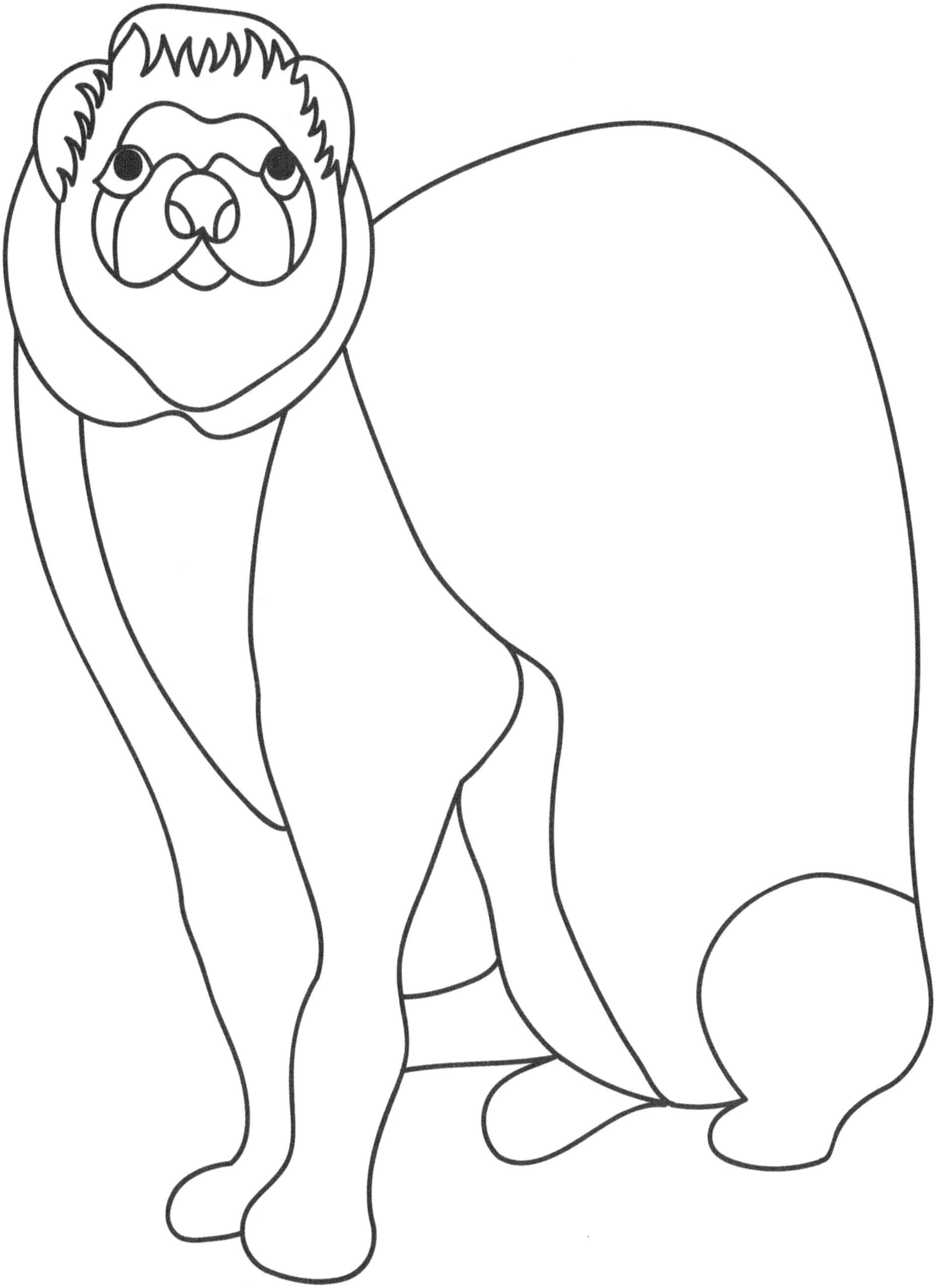

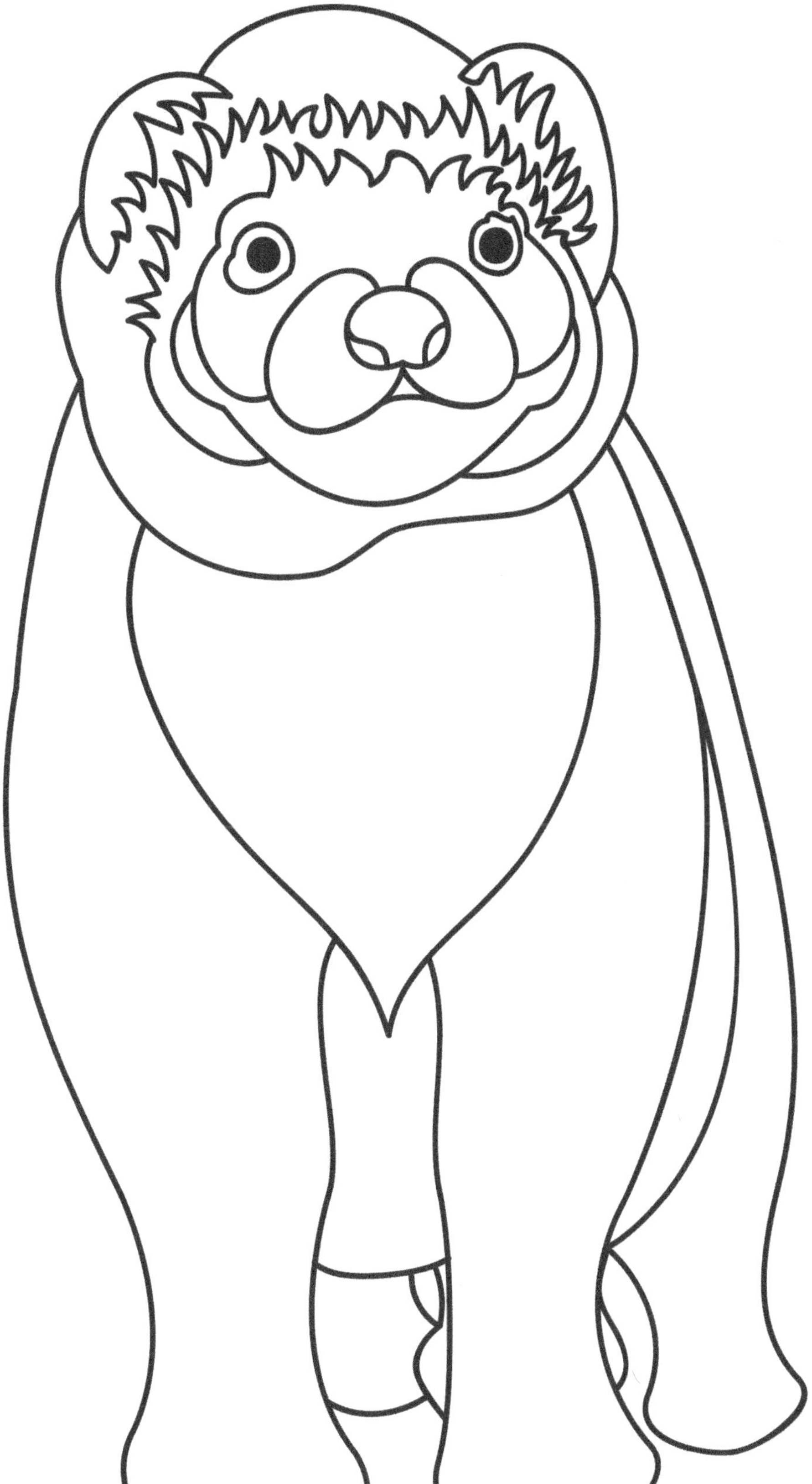

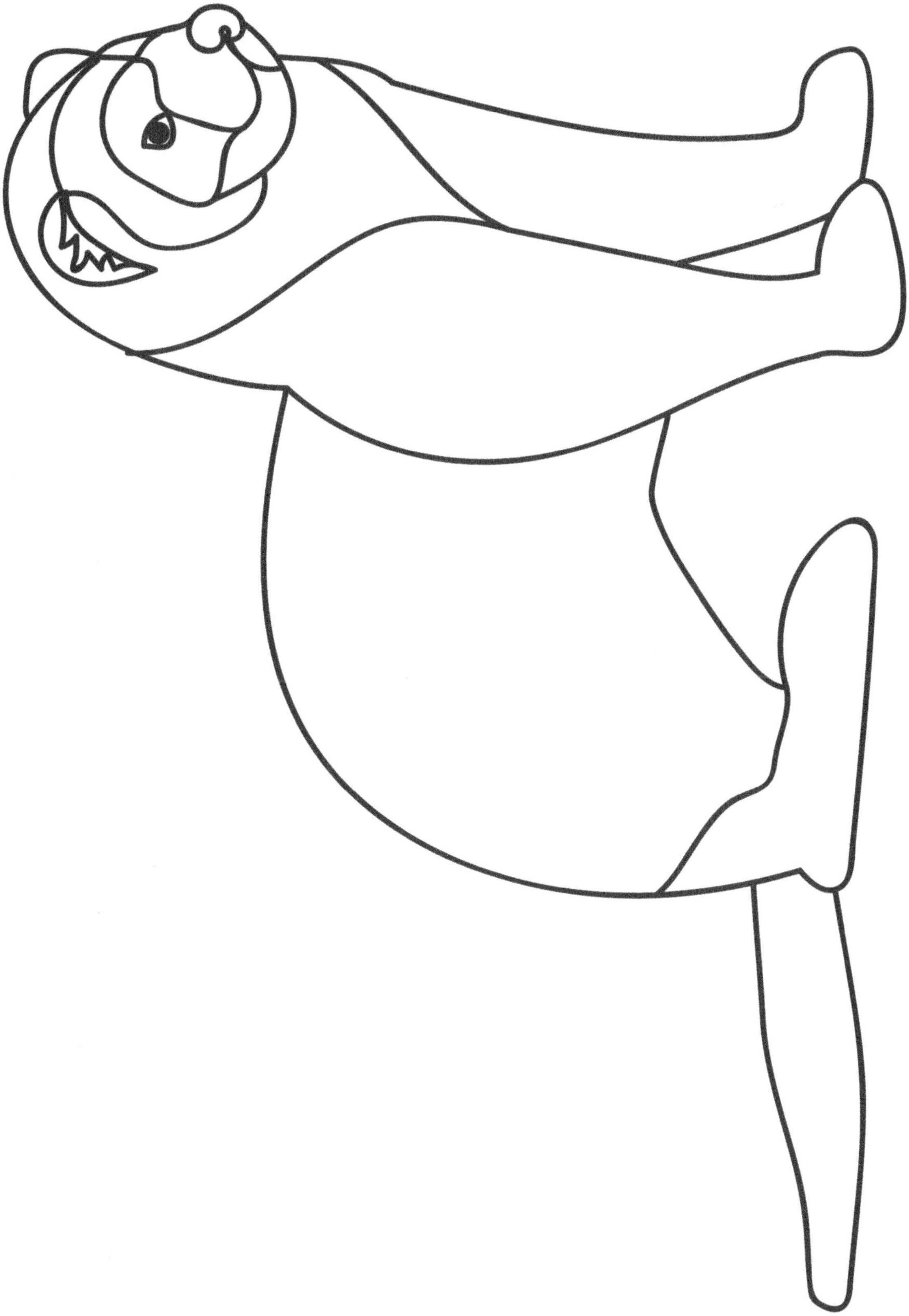

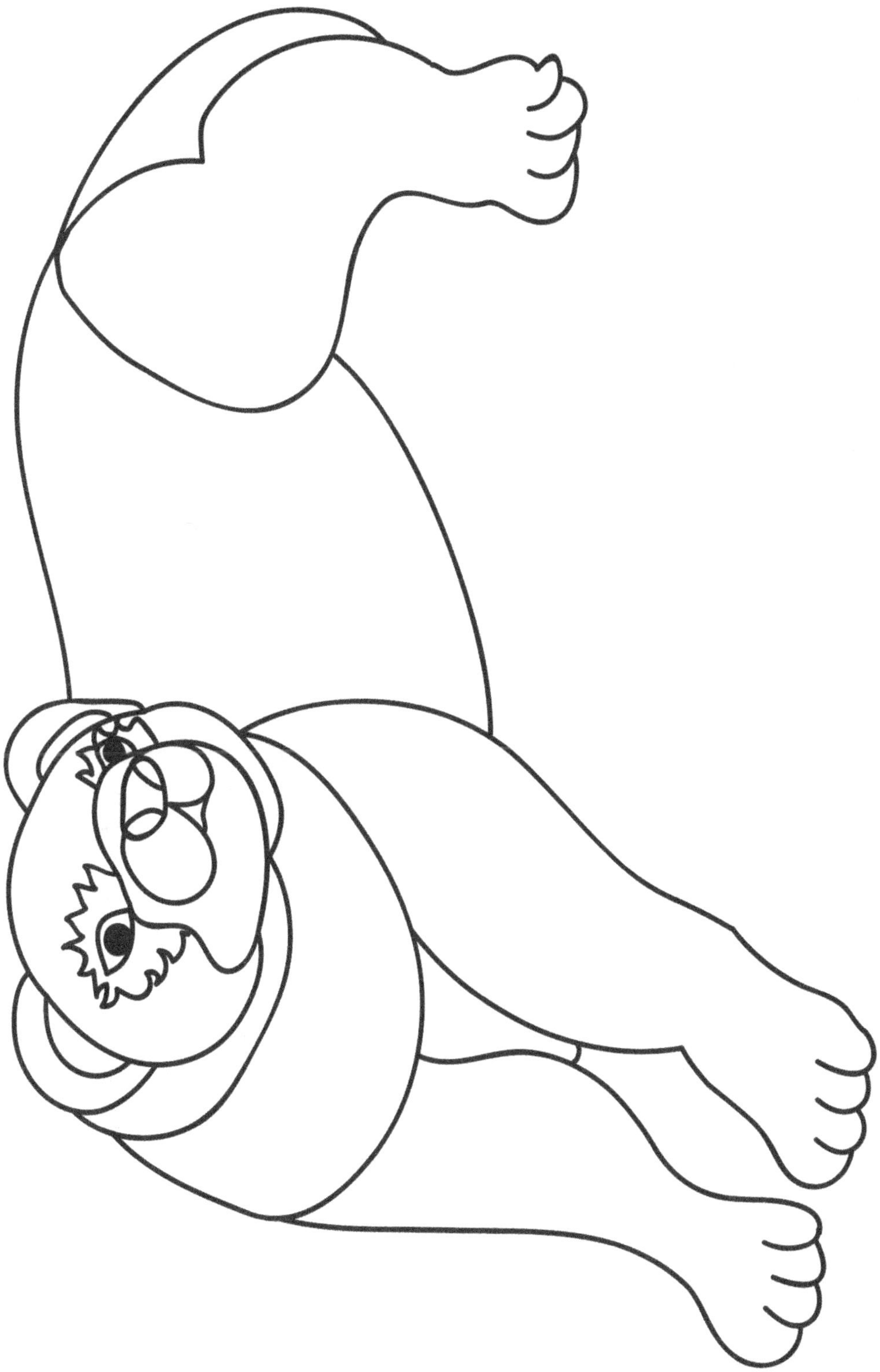

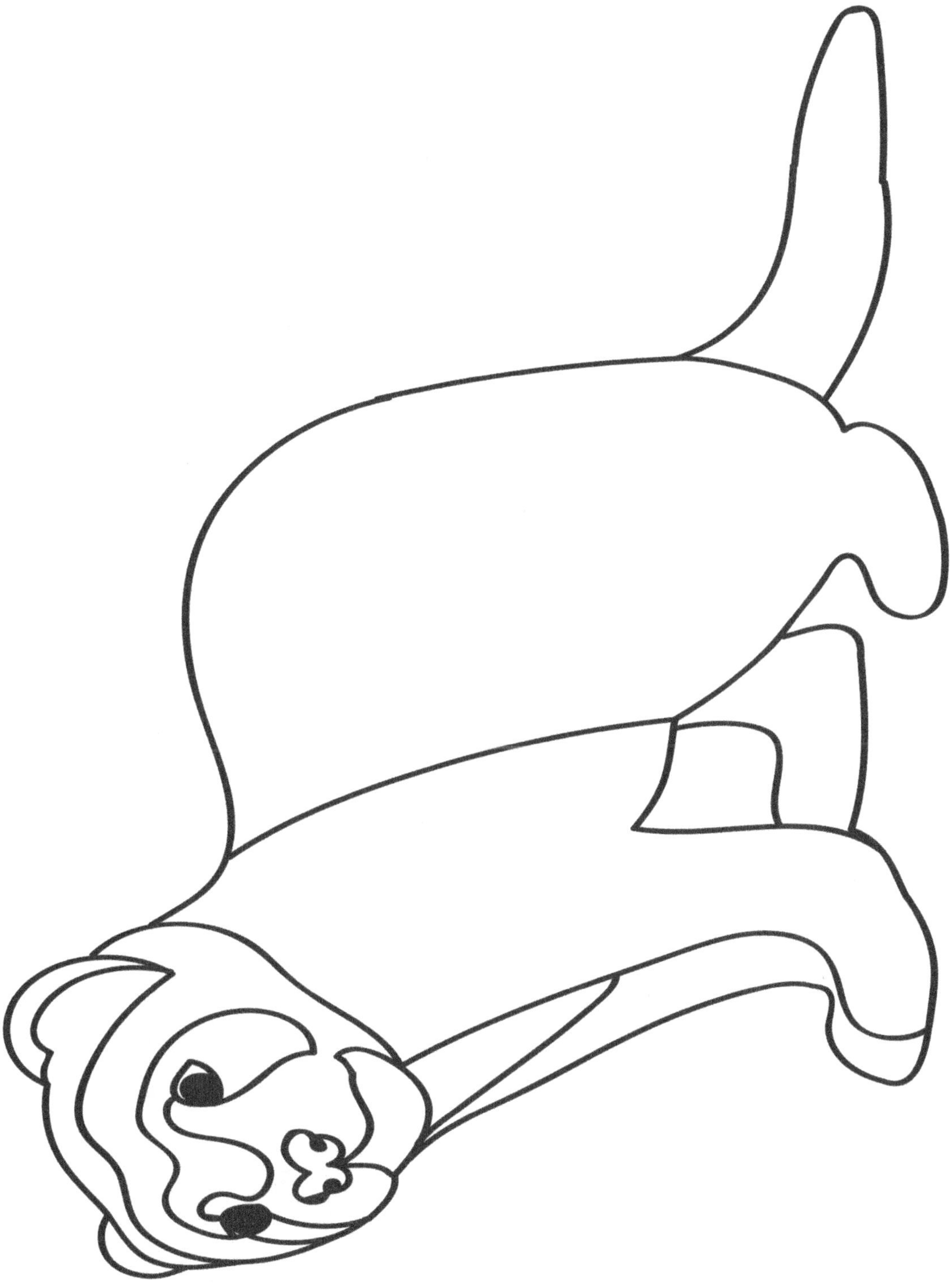

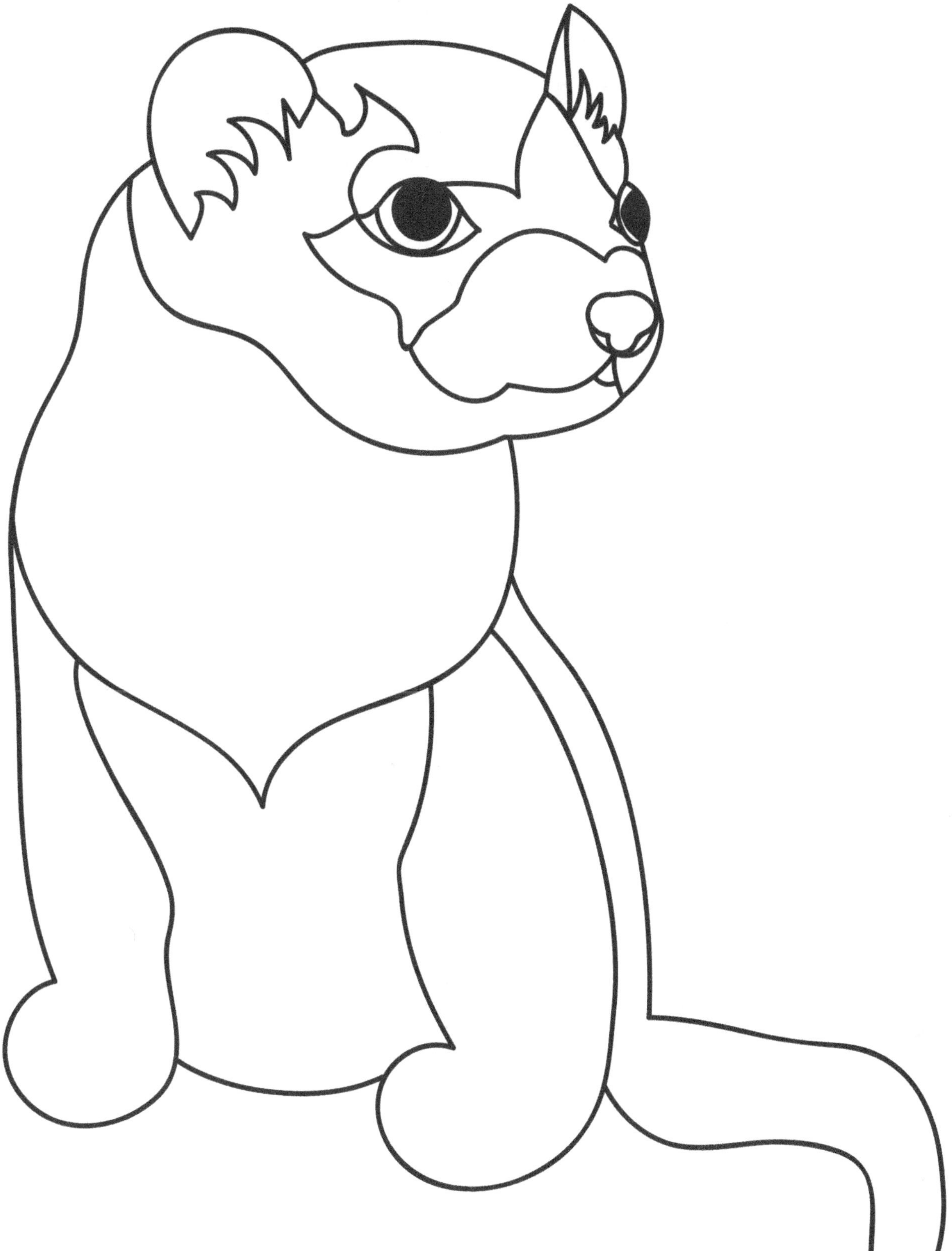

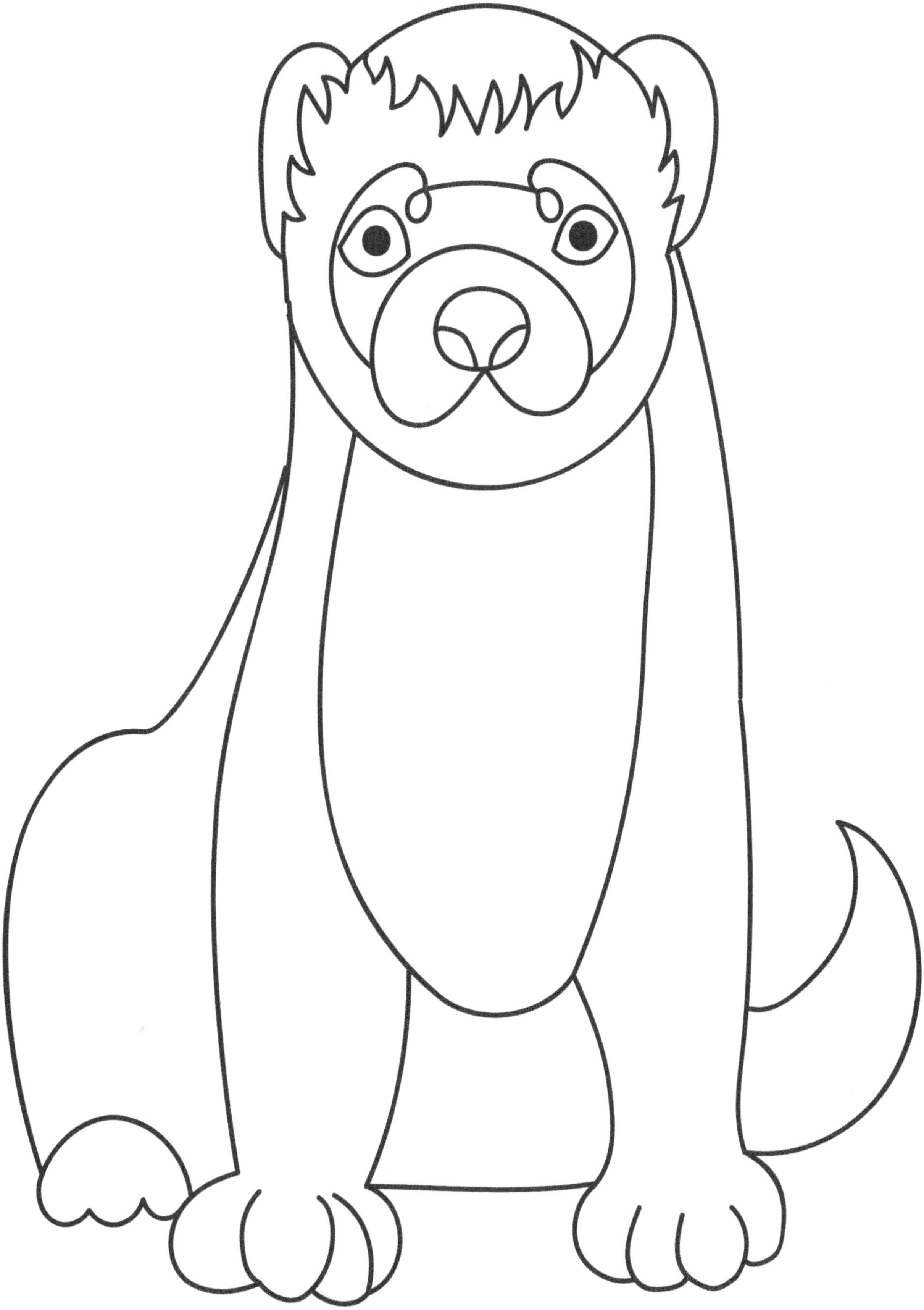

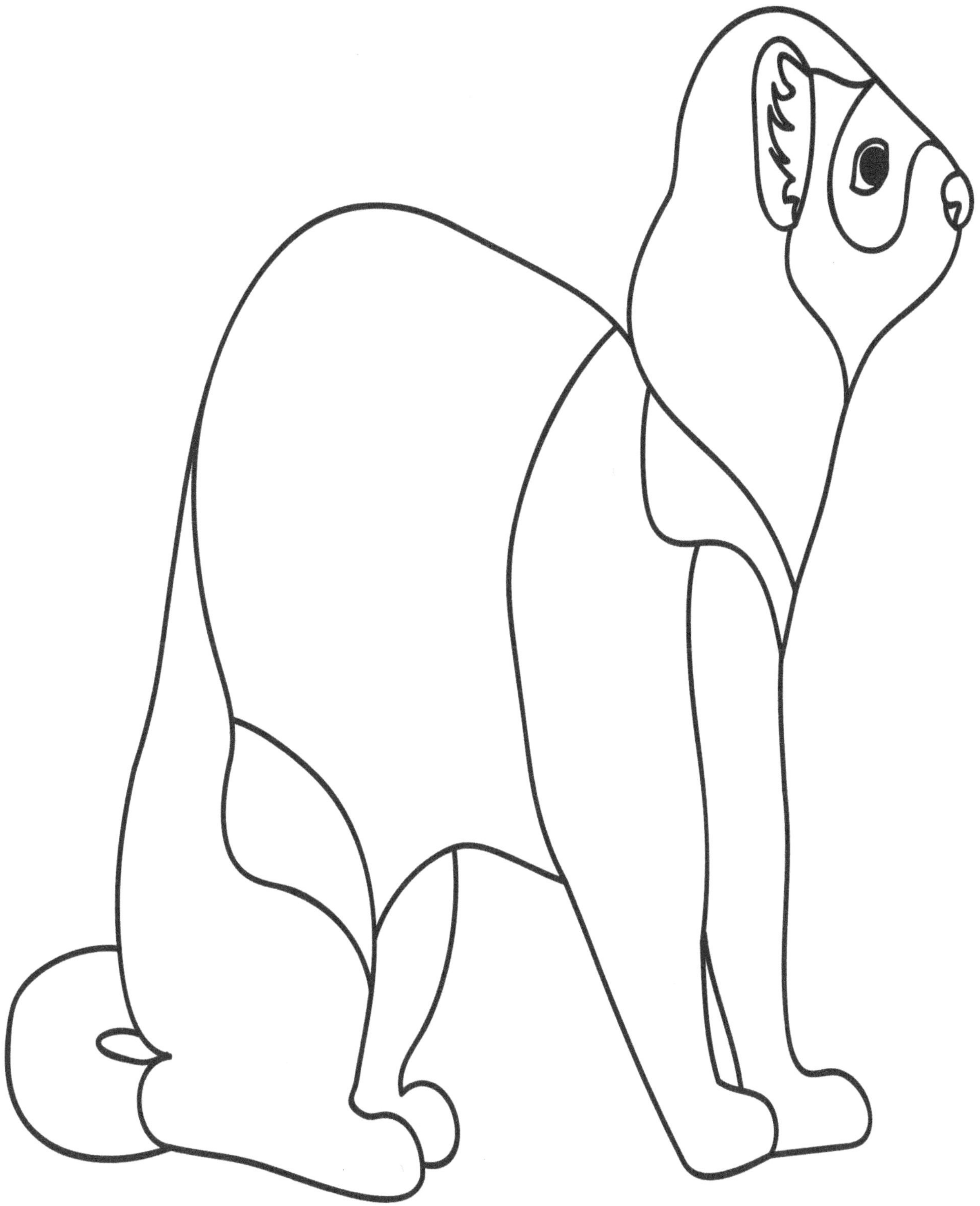

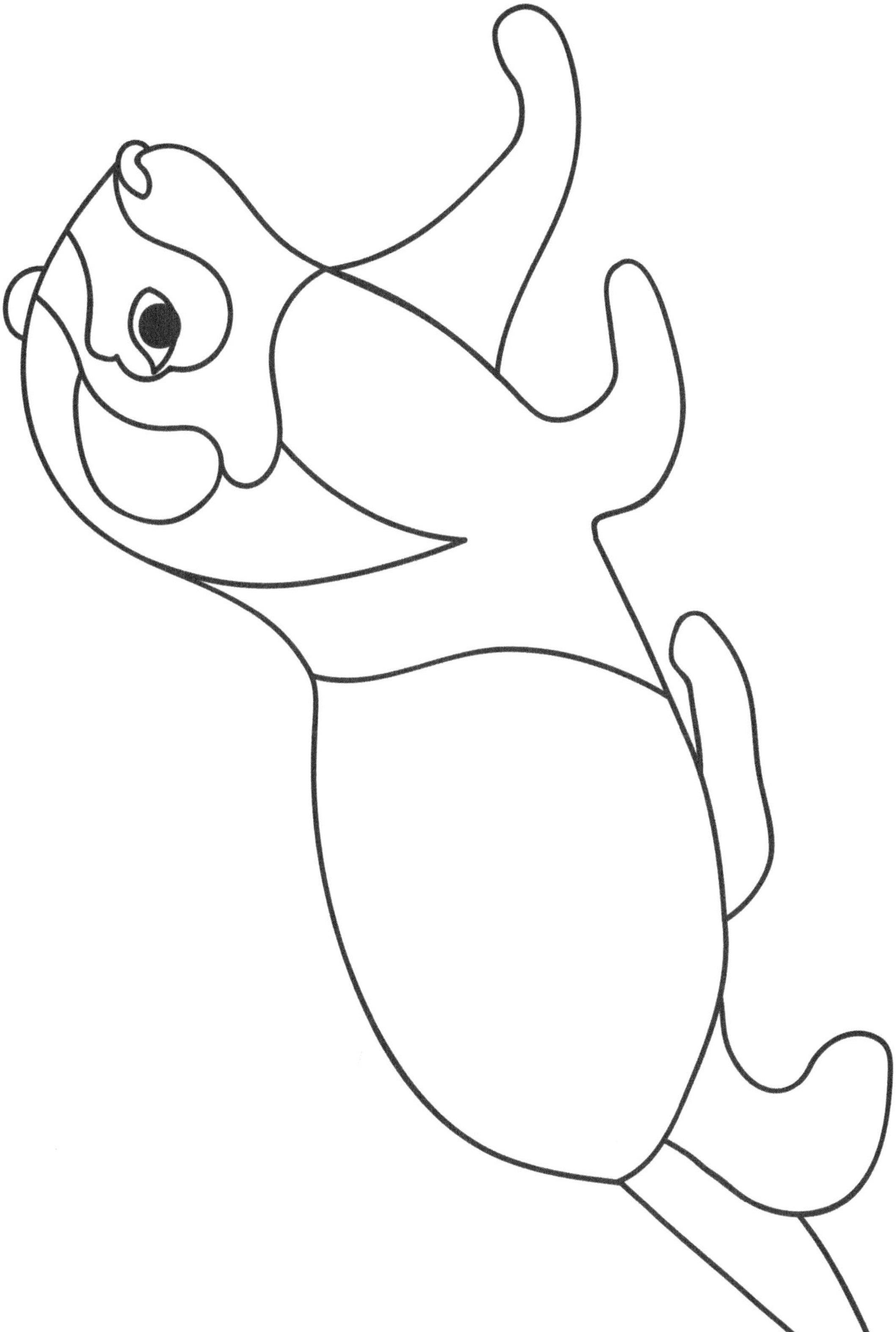

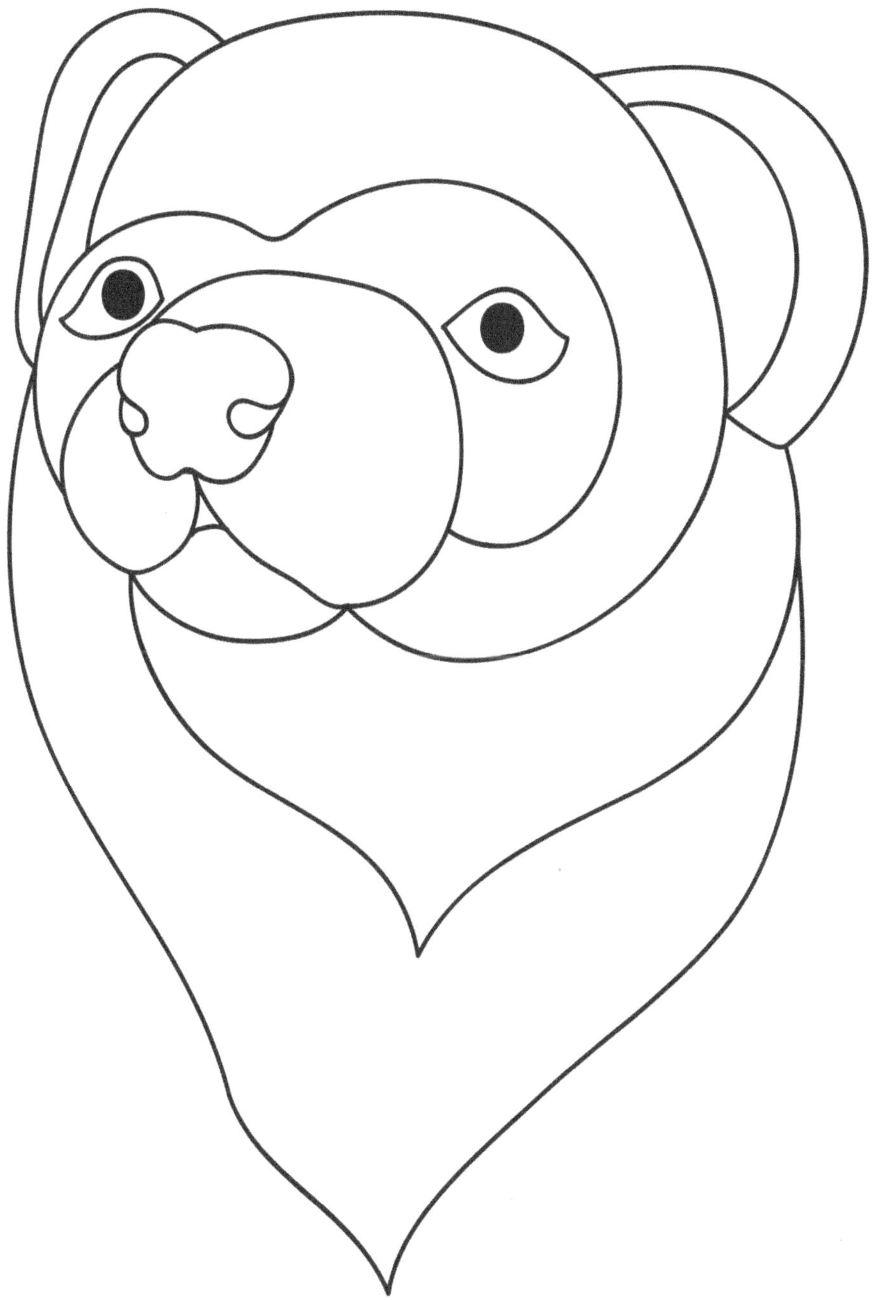

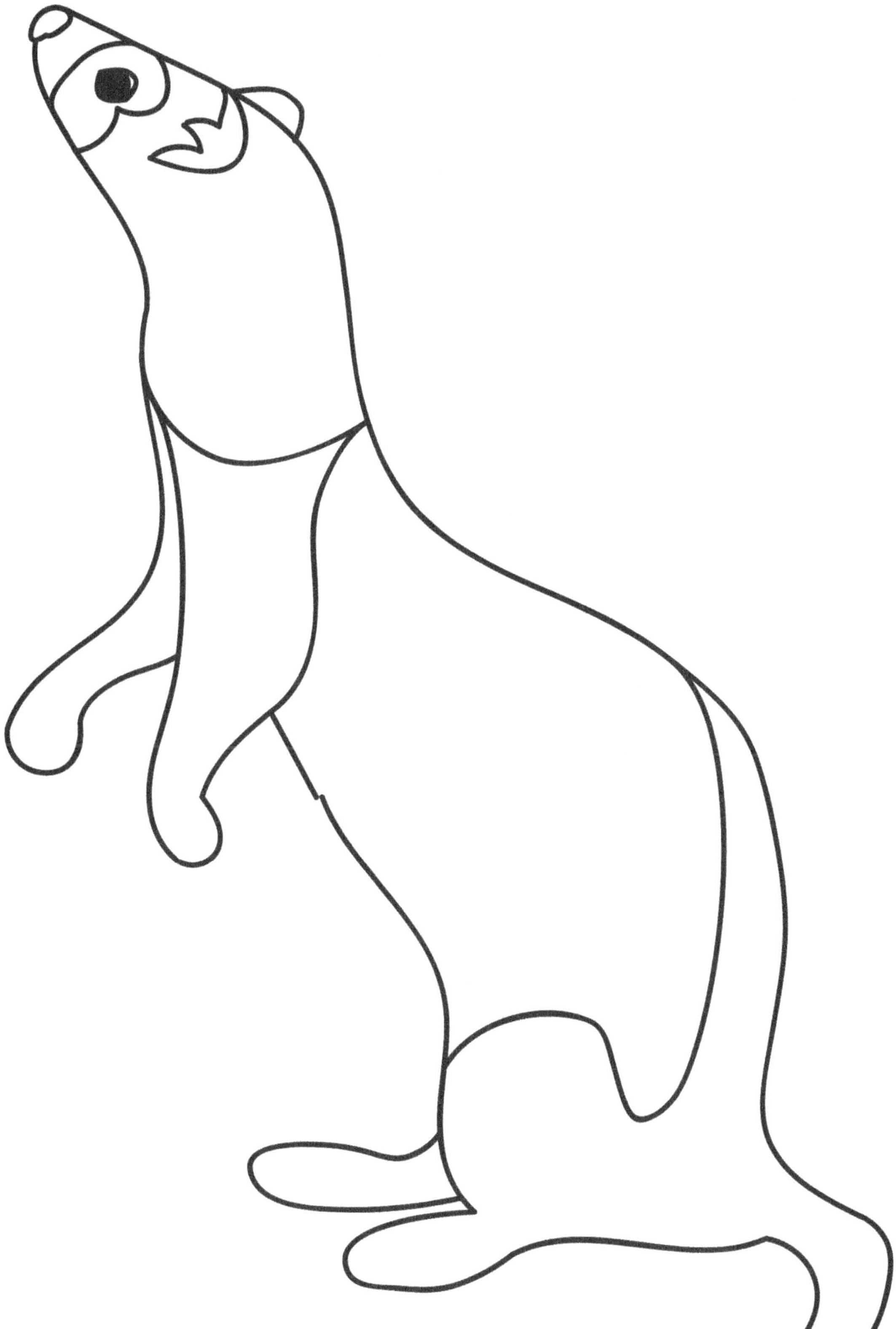

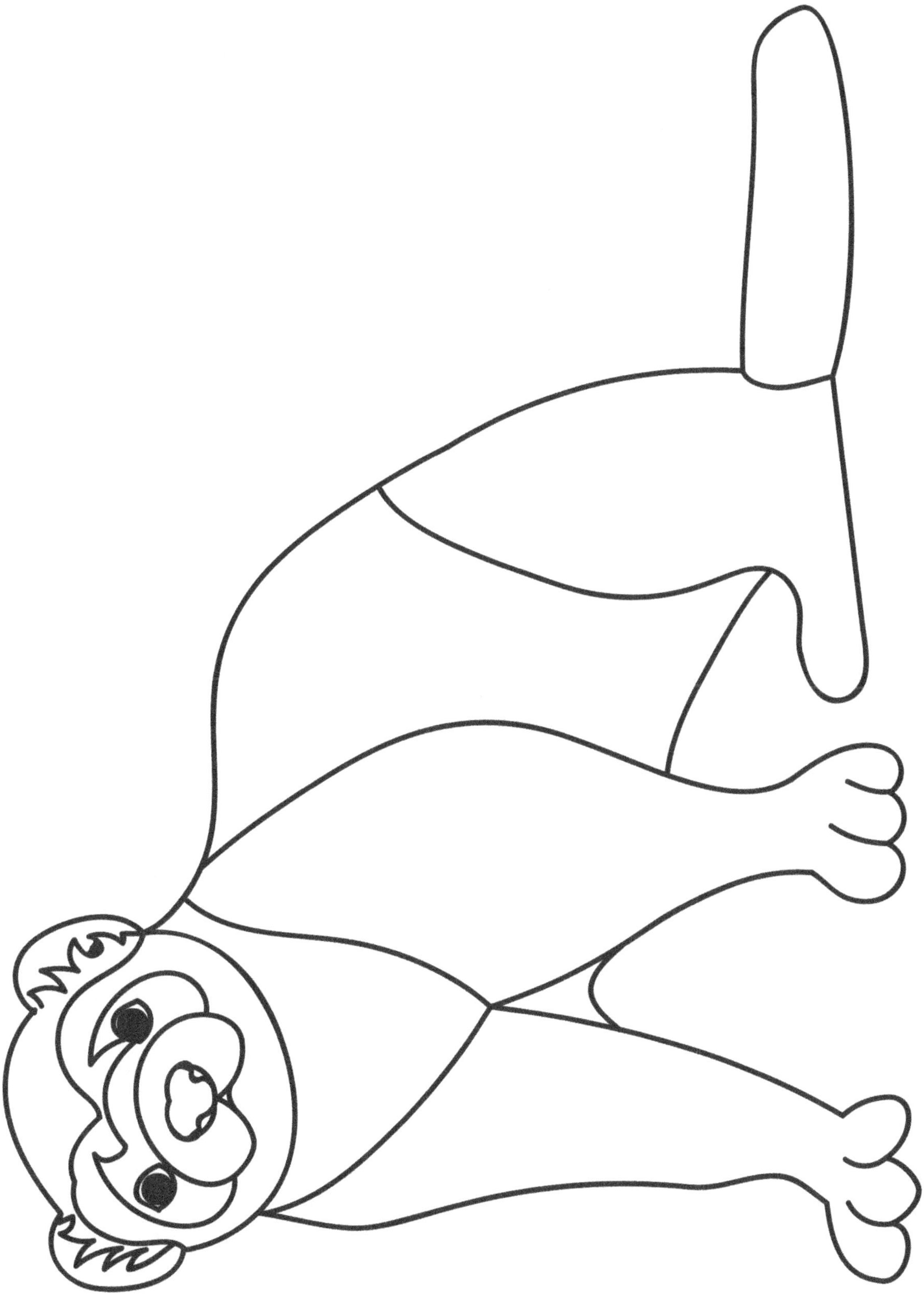

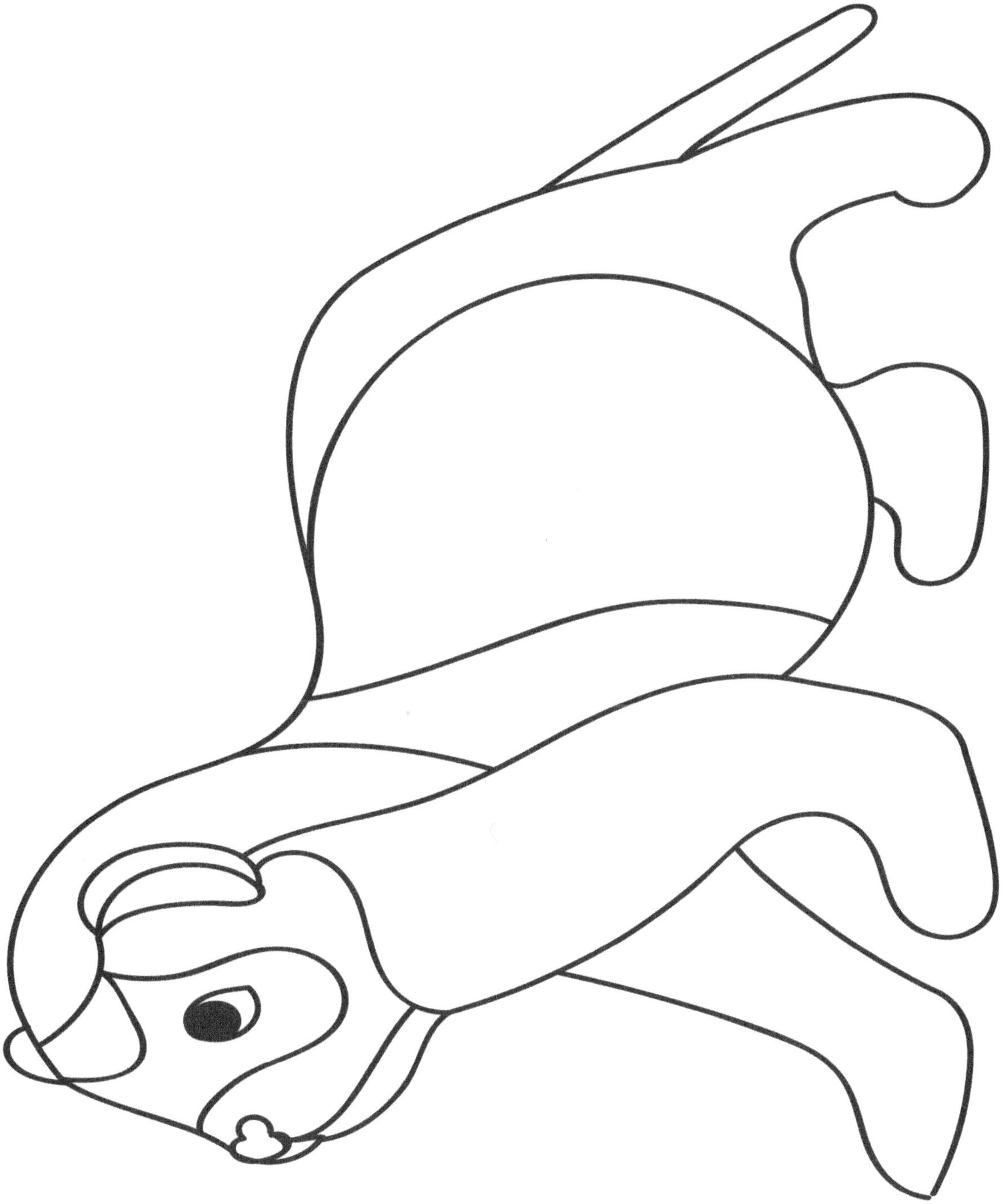

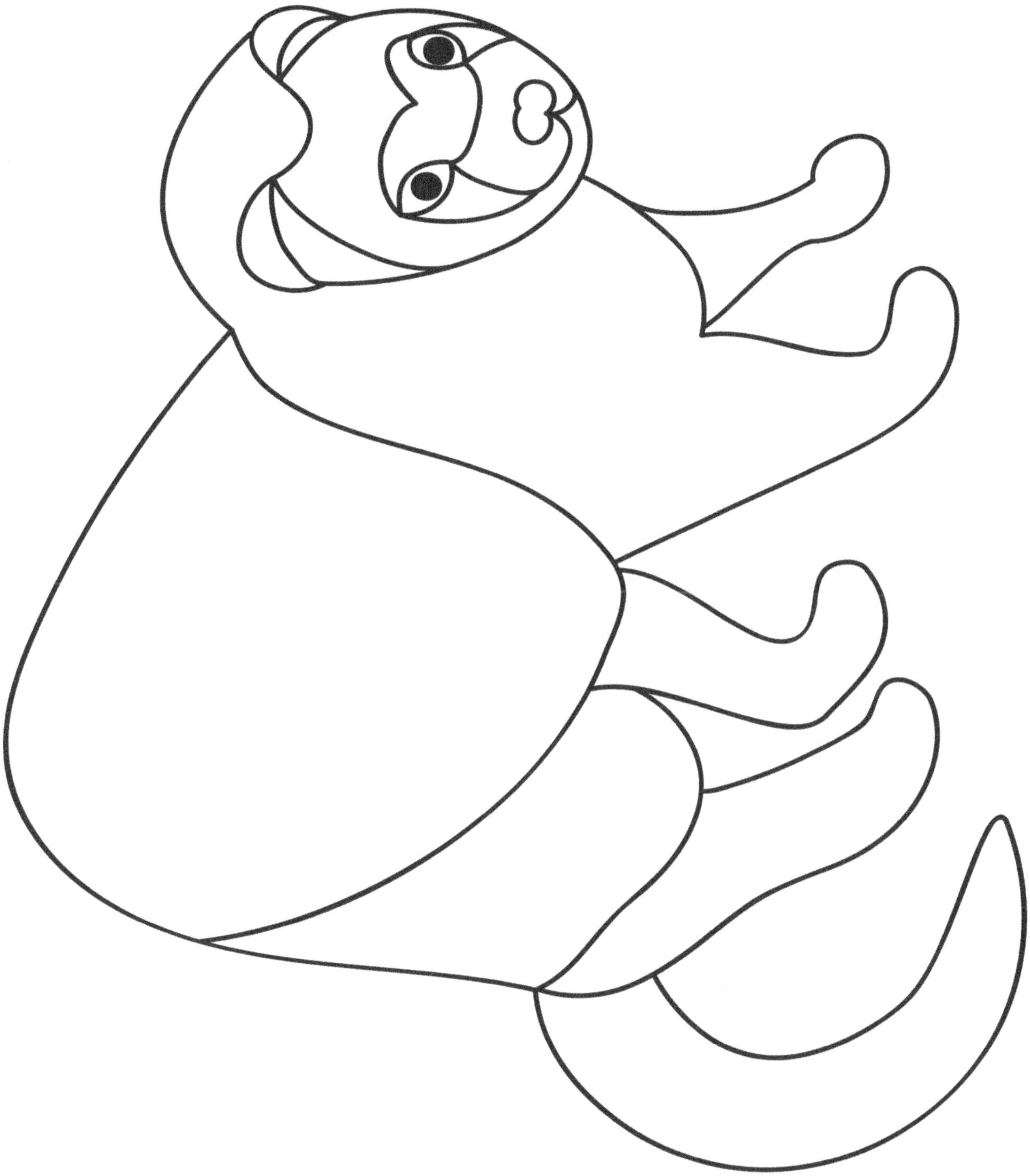

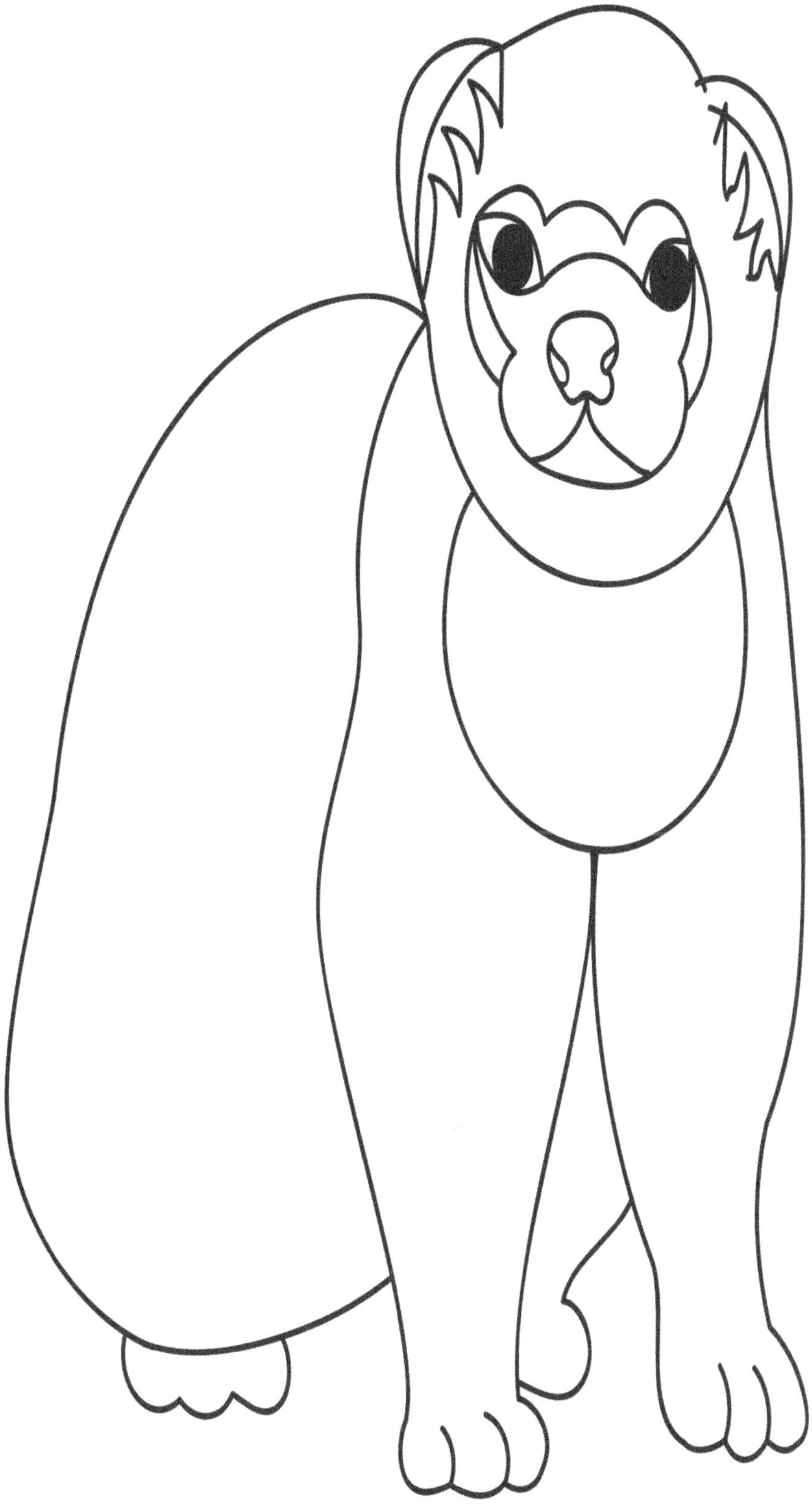

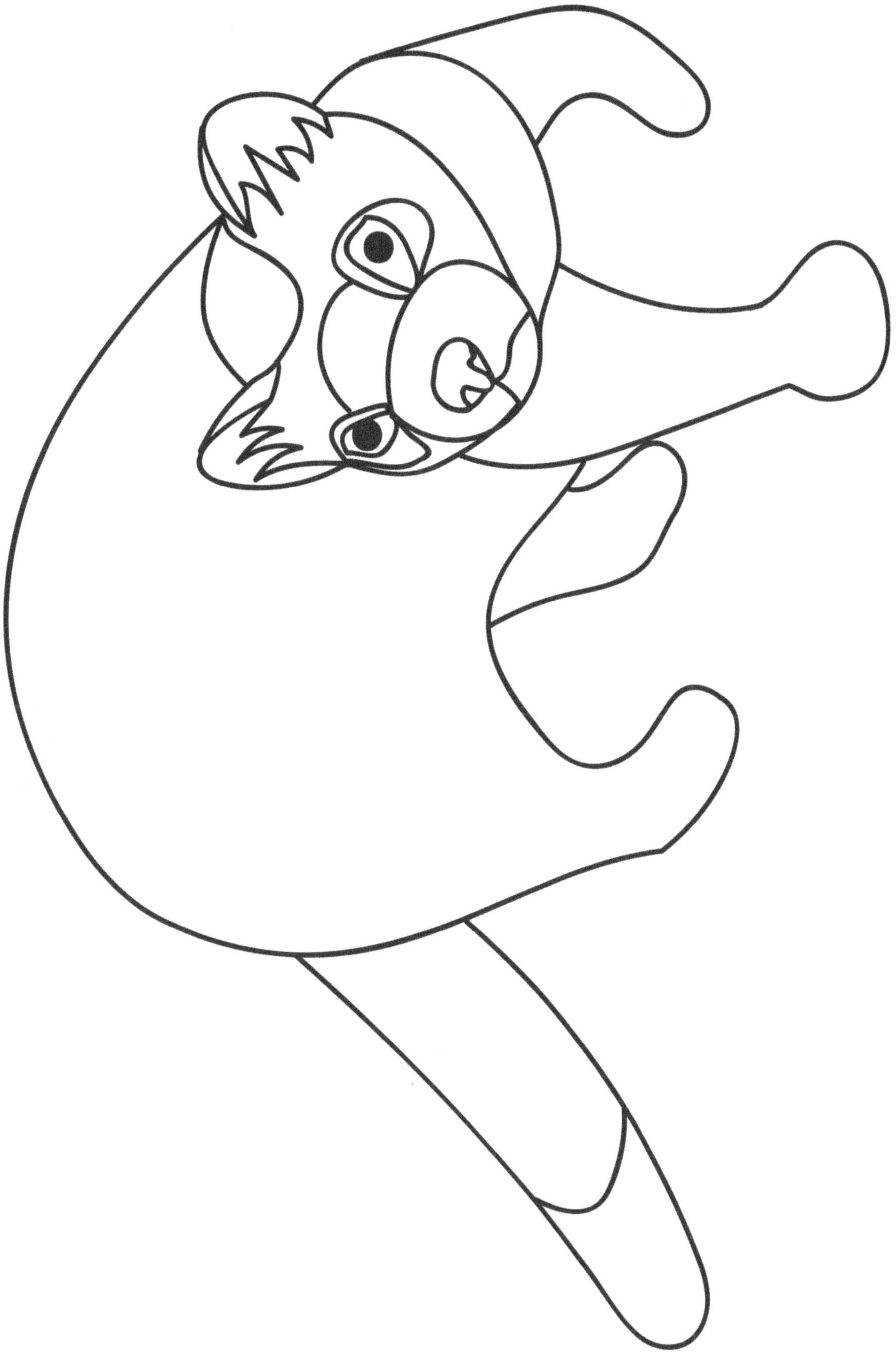

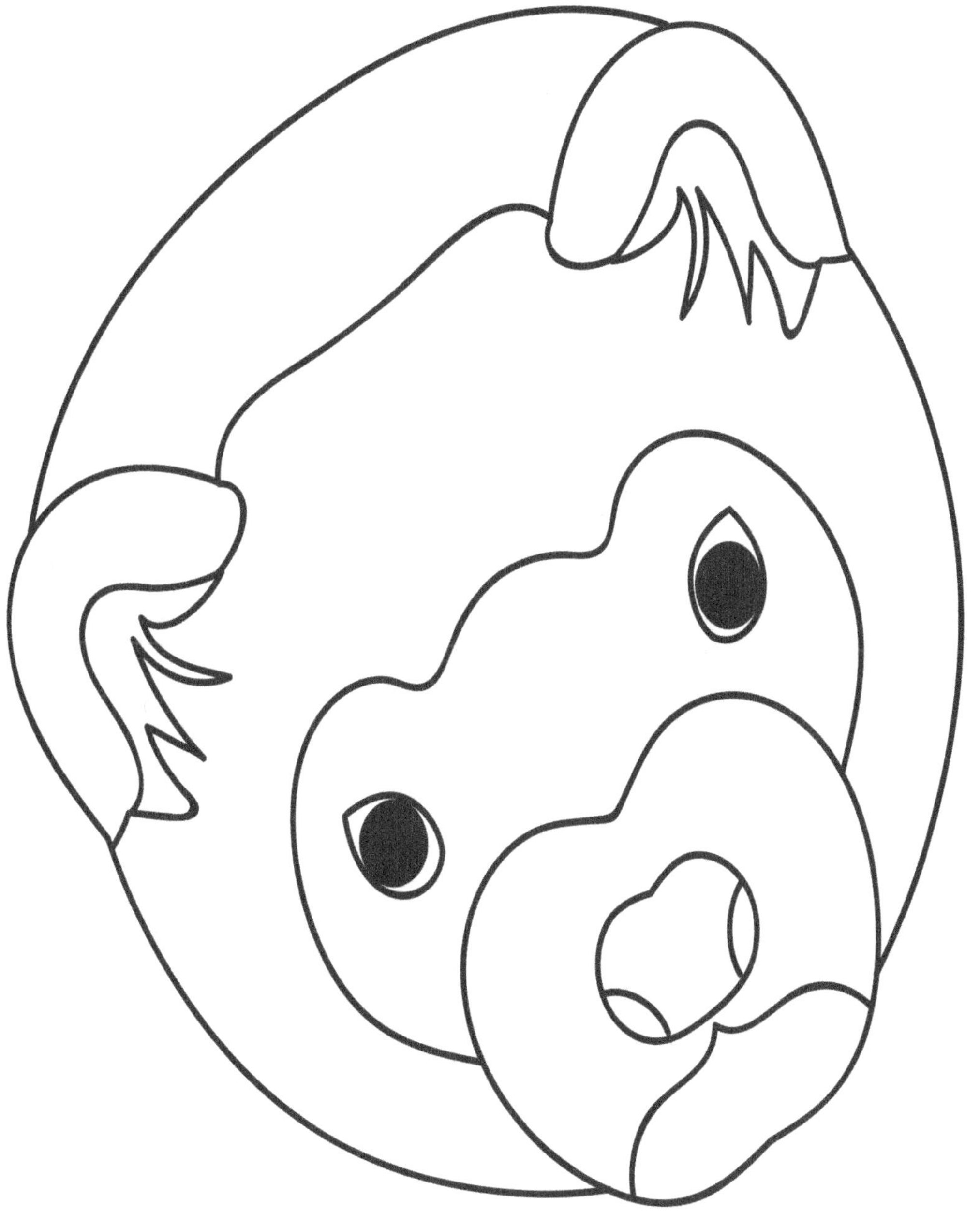

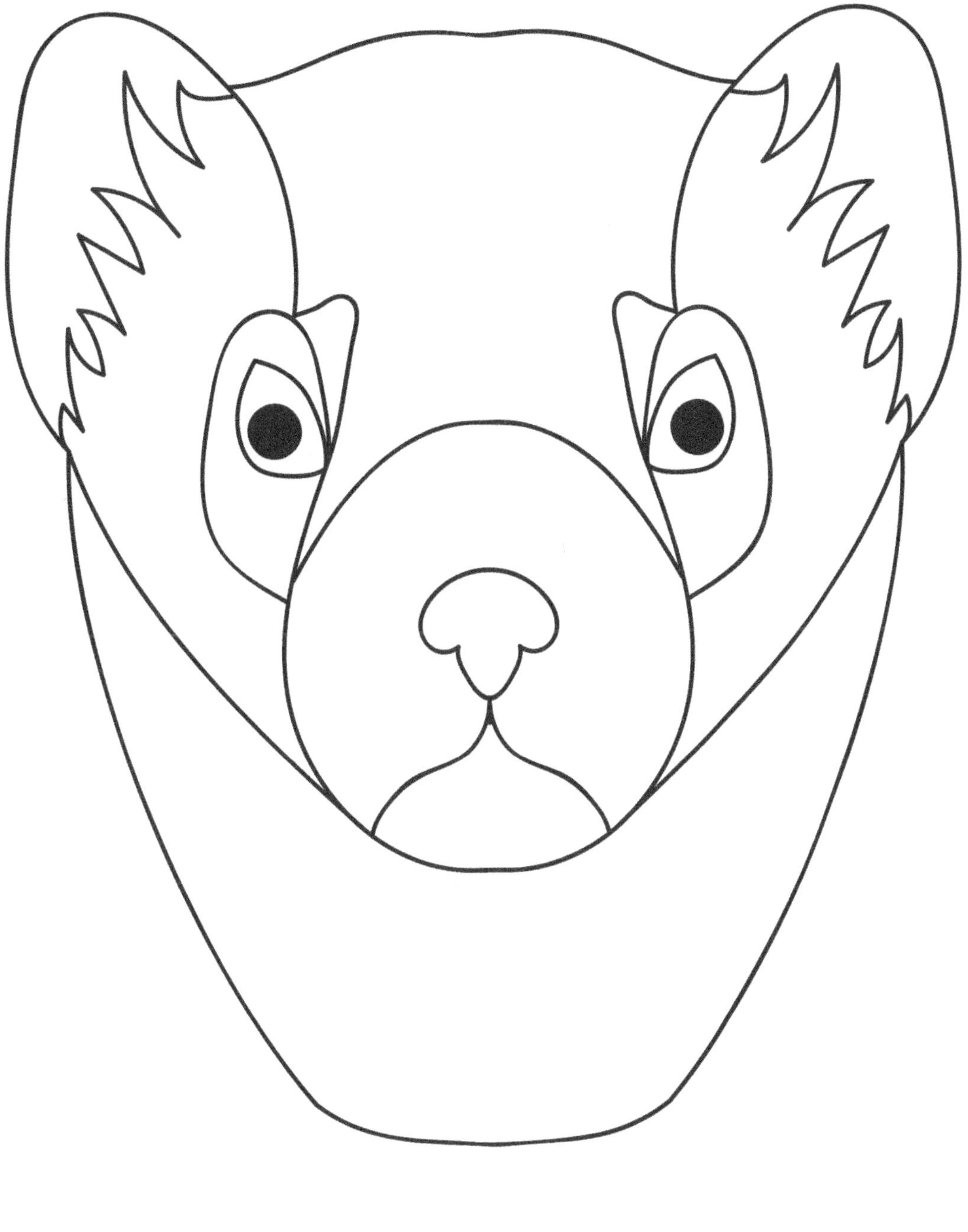

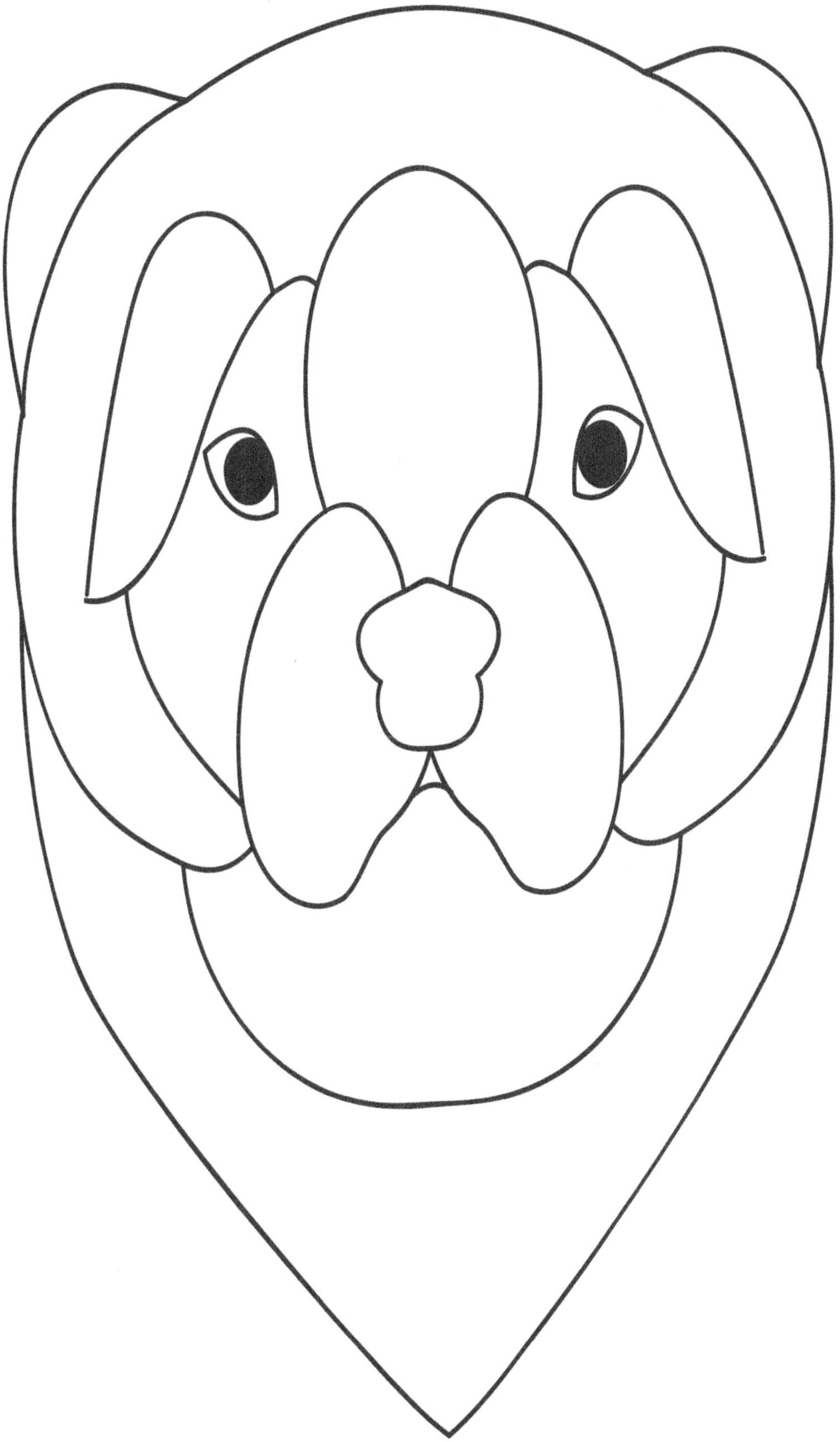

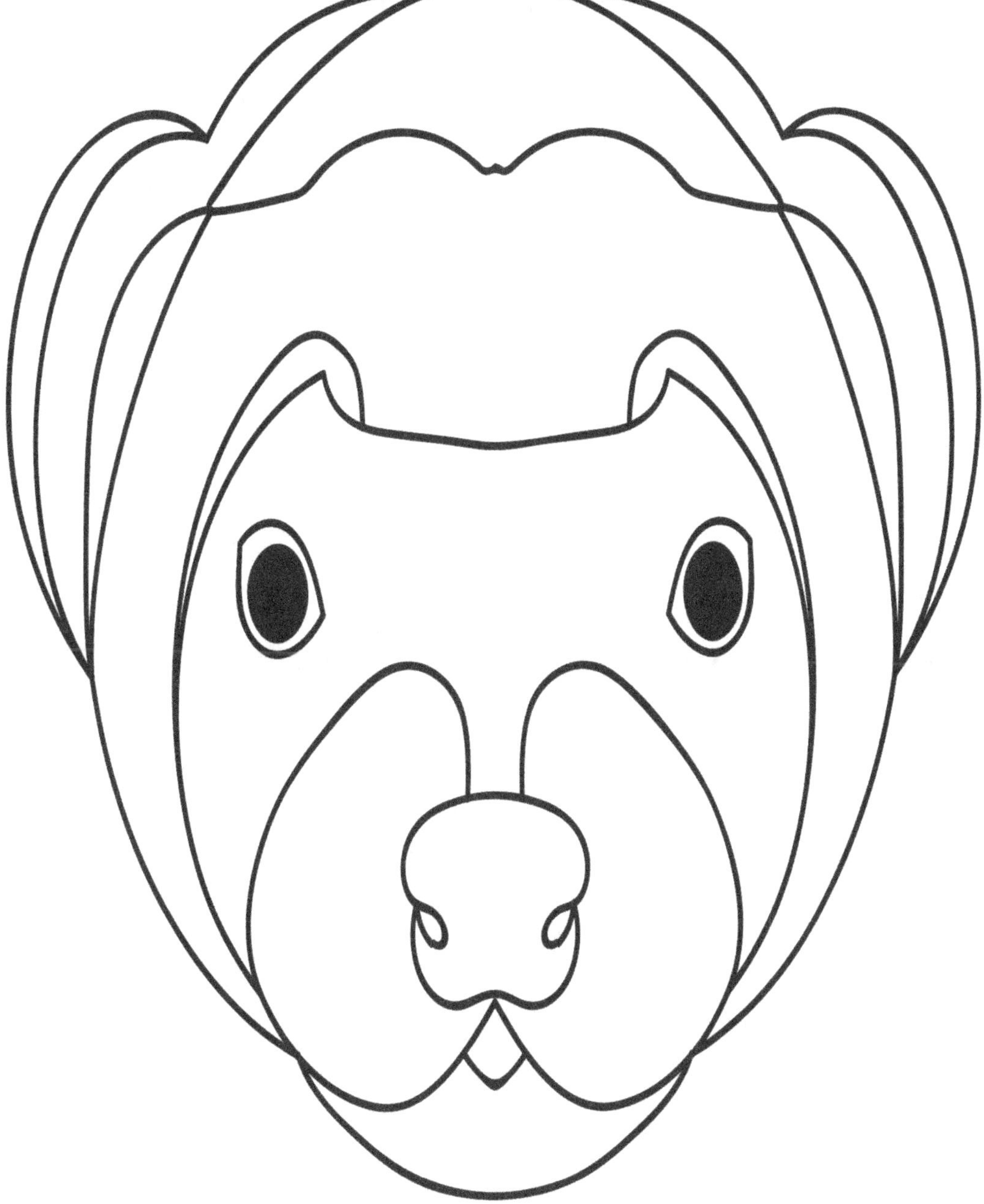

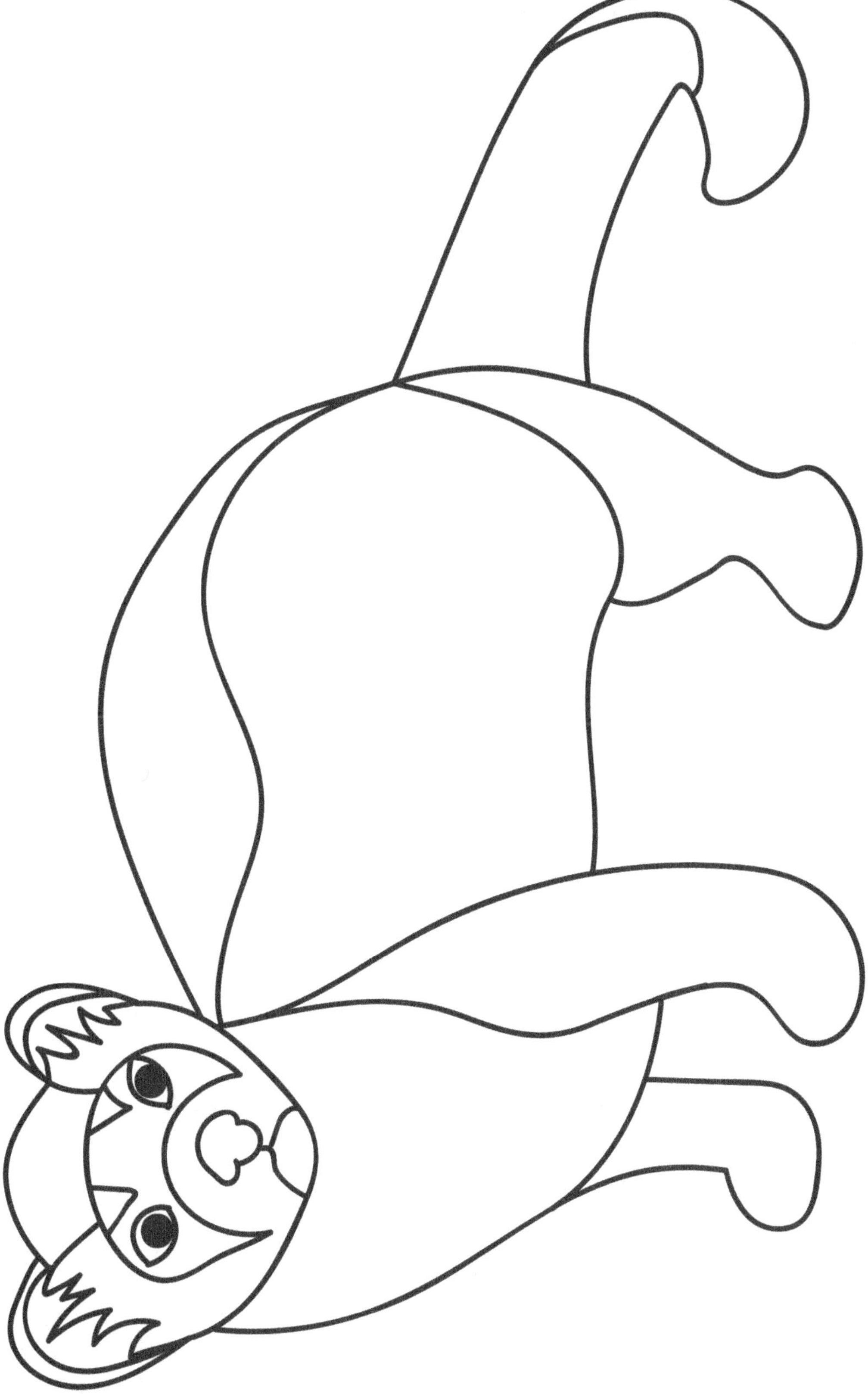

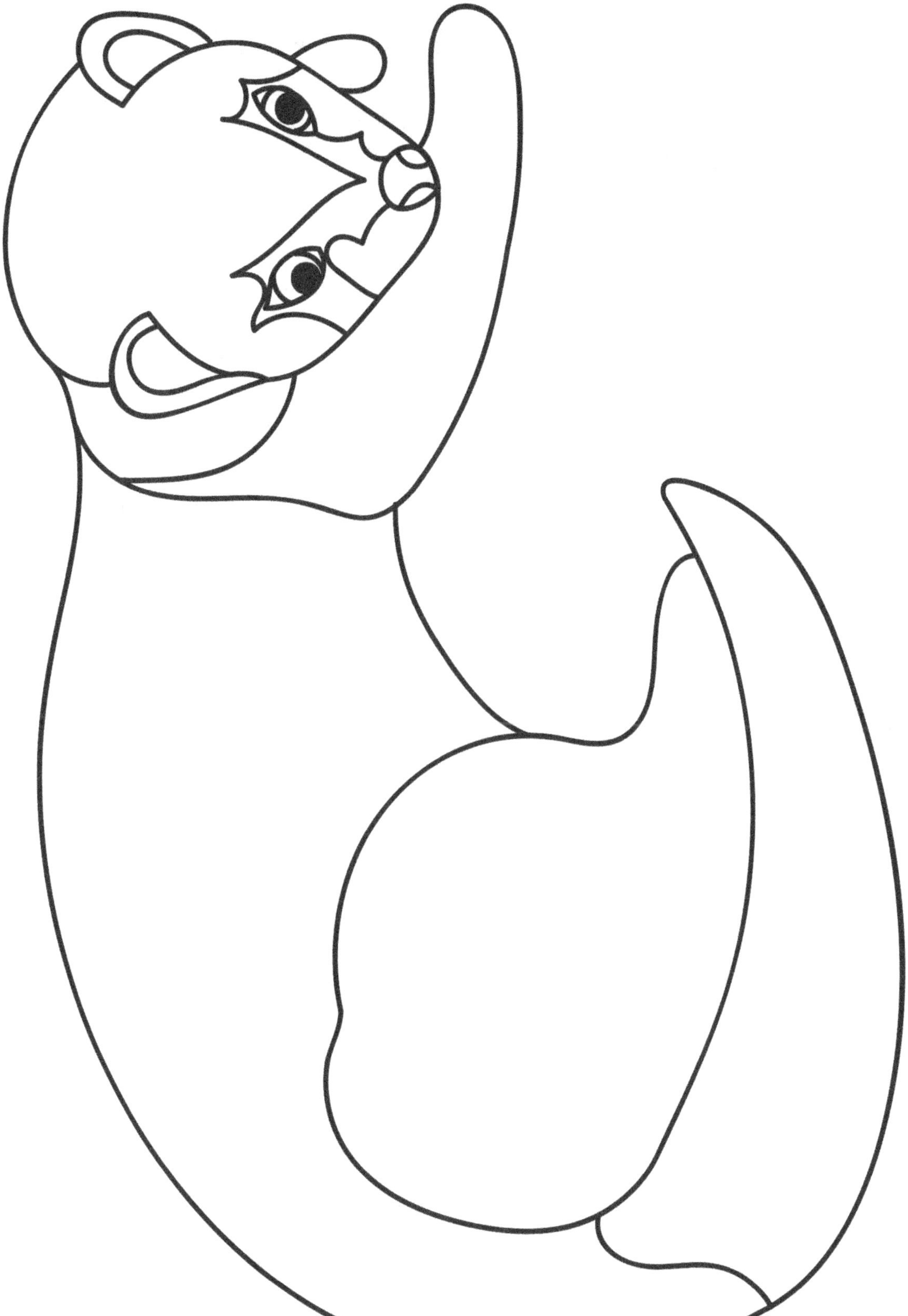

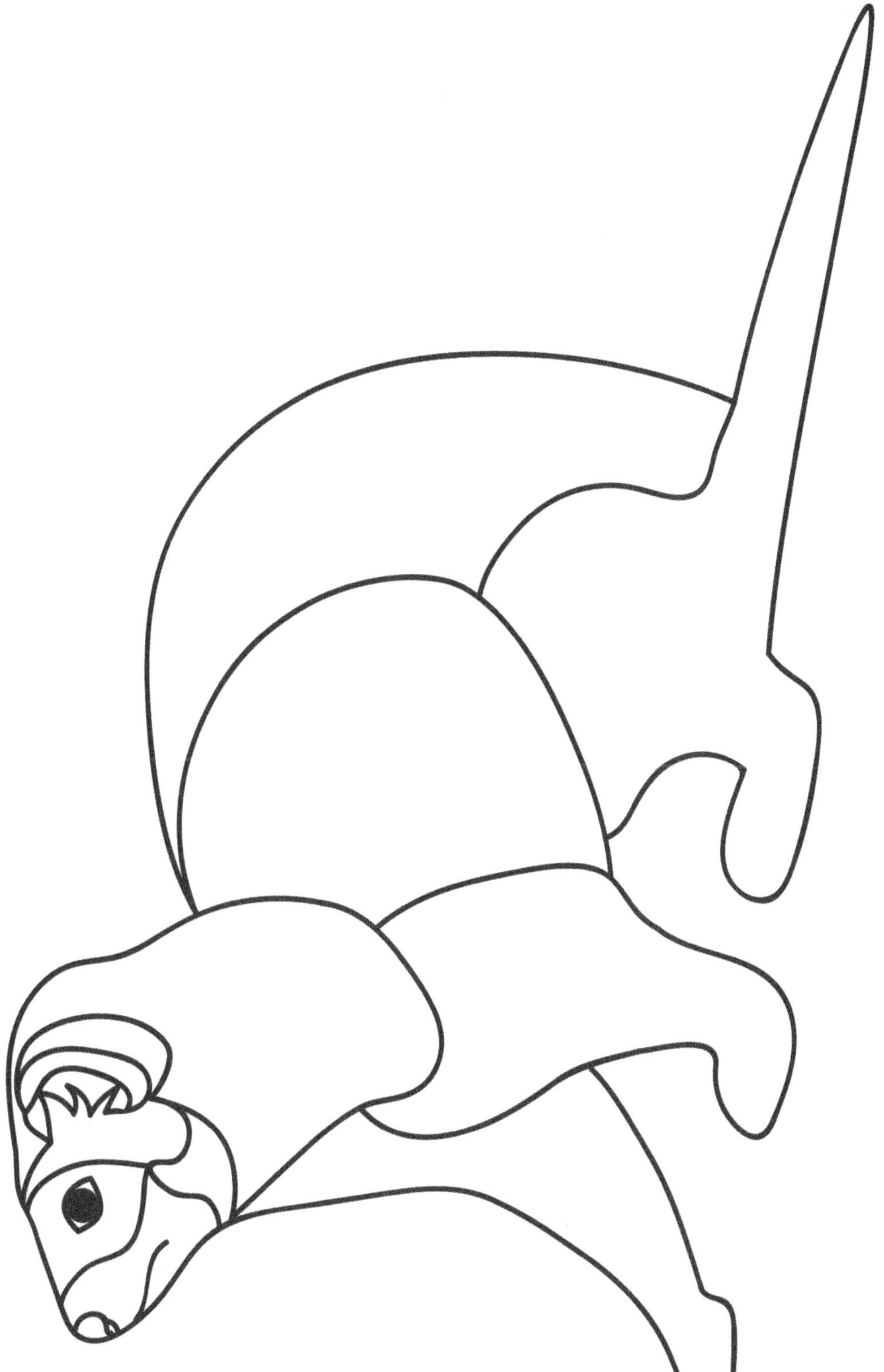

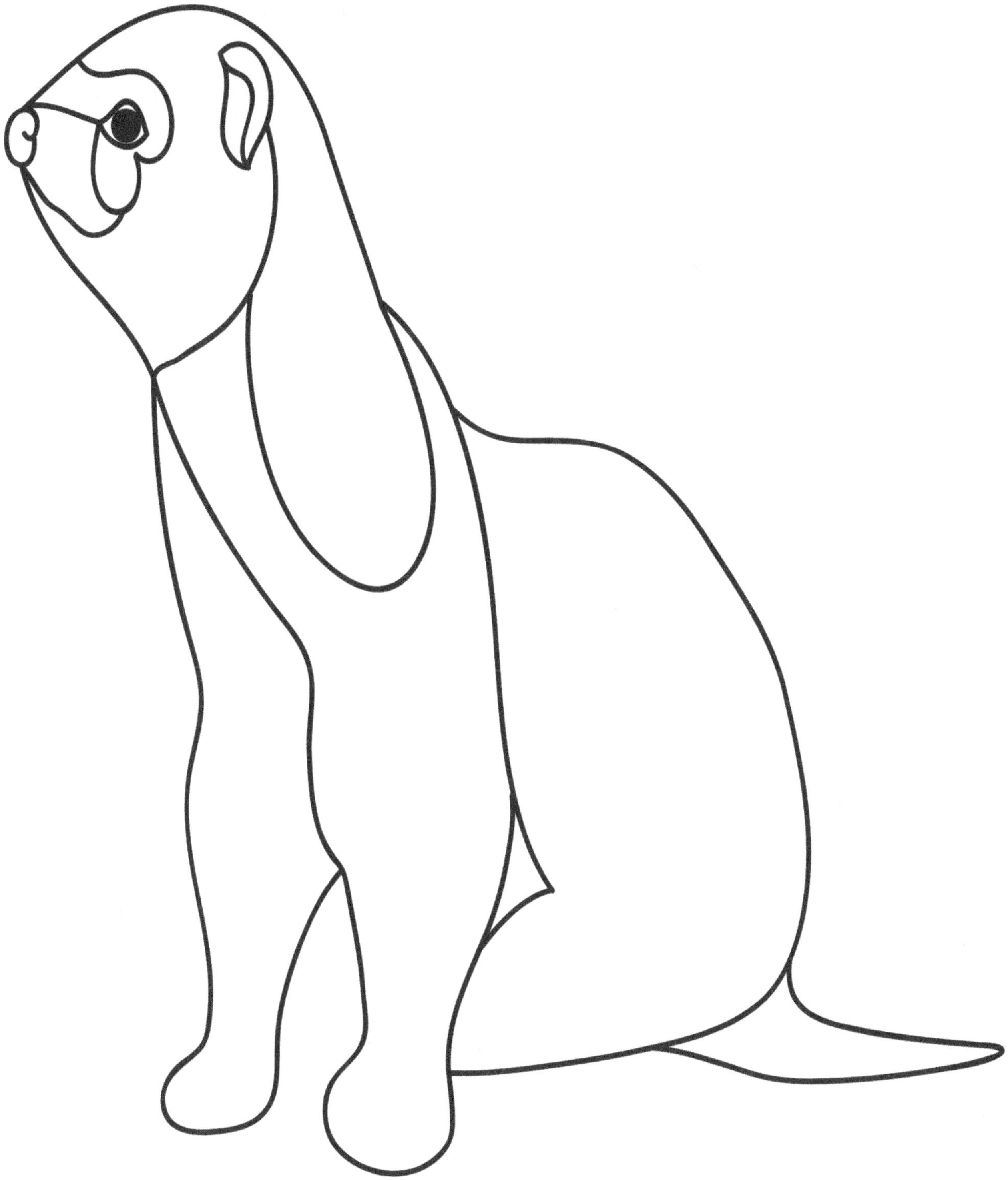

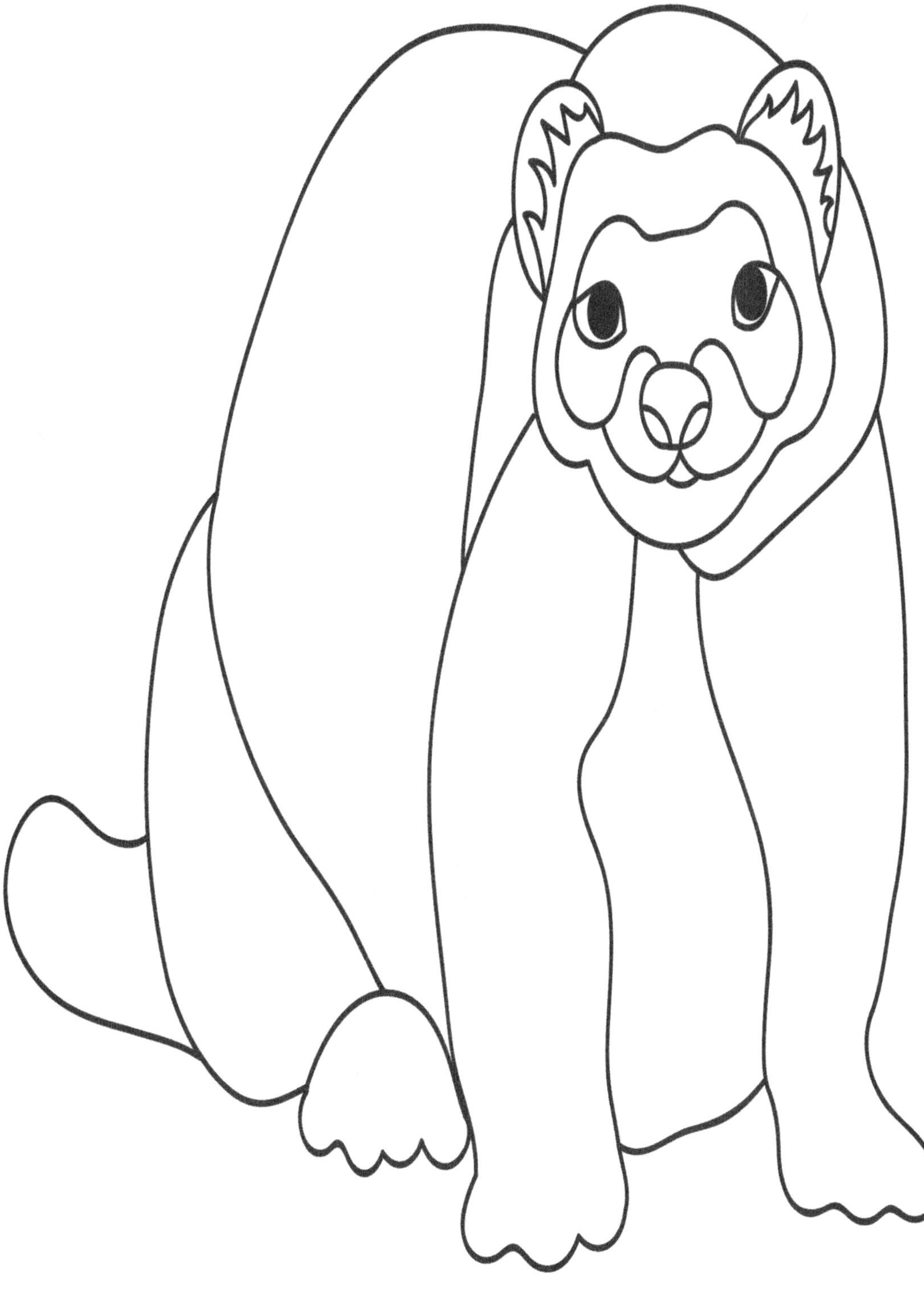

COLOR TEST PAGE

COLOR TEST PAGE

www.ingramcontent.com/pod-product-compliance
Lightning Source LLC
Chambersburg PA
CBHW062122220526
45471CB00010B/3840
* 9 7 8 1 9 8 7 6 4 7 1 8 1 *